Carving Canes & Walking Sticks

With Tom Wolfe

Text Written with and photography by Douglas Congdon-Martin

Schiffer Publishing Ltd

4880 Lower Valley Road · Atglen, PA 19310

ISBN: 978-0-88740-587-7
Printed in China

Published by Schiffer Publishing Ltd.
4880 Lower Valley Road
Atglen, PA 19310
Phone: (610) 593-1777; Fax: (610) 593-2002
E-mail: Info@schifferbooks.com

For the largest selection of fine reference books on this and related subjects, please visit our website at
www.schifferbooks.com
We are always looking for people to write books on new and related subjects. If you have an idea for a book, please contact us at the above address.

This book may be purchased from the publisher.
Include $5.00 for shipping.
Please try your bookstore first.
You may write for a free catalog.

In Europe, Schiffer books are distributed by
Bushwood Books
6 Marksbury Ave.
Kew Gardens
Surrey TW9 4JF England
Phone: 44 (0) 20 8392 8585; Fax: 44 (0) 20 8392 9876
E-mail: info@bushwoodbooks.co.uk
Website: www.bushwoodbooks.co.uk

Contents

Introduction

They're as beautiful as they are functional. Perhaps that is why there is such a fascination these days with canes and walking sticks. What was once thought of as a quaint artifact of days gone by, when a man was not properly attired without a cane, now is experiencing a resurgence.

Some of this is due to the growing number of campers who take to the trails each weekend. Their walking sticks are an important part of their gear, giving them a boost on steep terrain, or simply adding a pleasant beat to their walking.

In the city, more and more people are experiencing the sense of security a cane provides. It is something to hold onto in an environment that is sometimes hostile.

City slickers and country cousins alike find their "sticks" to be an object that expresses their personality in a very intimate way. The shape, size, design, and color all say something about who they are.

I guess that's why I have always had so many people interested in the canes and walking sticks I make. If I had wanted to, I probably could have spent my whole time carving them for people...and made a good living at it to boot. There is no end to the kinds of carving you can do on these sticks. Each one is as unique as the person who will use it.

I have included eleven patterns in this book. This should give you a good start...but don't stop here. Experiment with your own patterns and have a great time!

Carving the Wooden Handle Cane

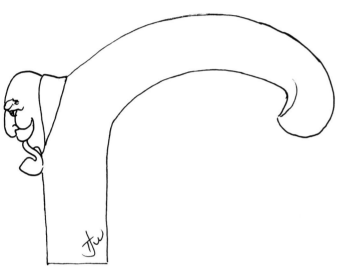

All patterns reduced to **65 %**.
Enlarge to **155%** for original size.

You need to drill a hole for this connecting threaded rod. The easiest way to do this is on a drill press.

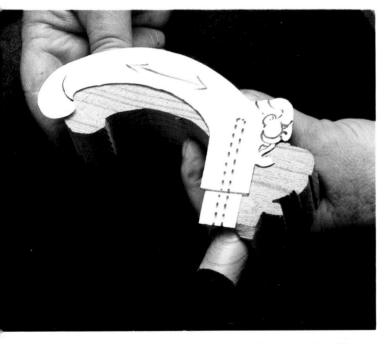

Cut the handle blank from stock that is 11/4 inches thick. The grain needs to runs through the handle.

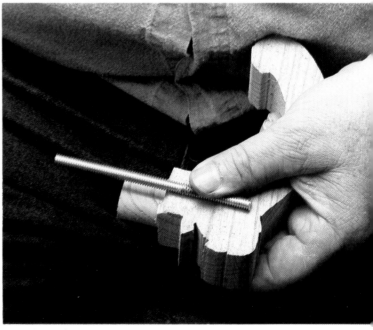

The knob is cut with a hole cutter, using the hole you just drilled as a guide. Again use a drill press.

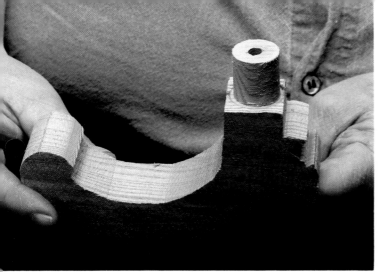

The result.

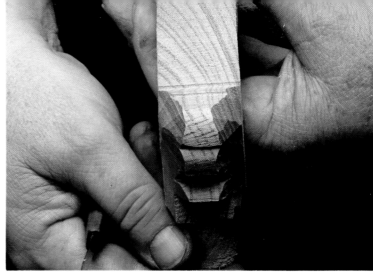

This should take you to this stage.

Knock the corners off the face.

With a curved cut begin to take away beside the nose.

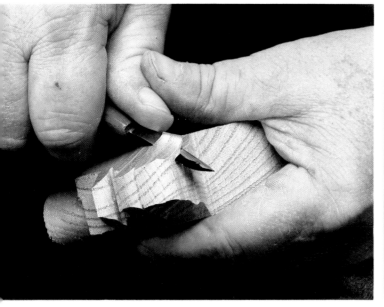

Continue to the top of the head.

Before going too much further, I'd better draw a center line.

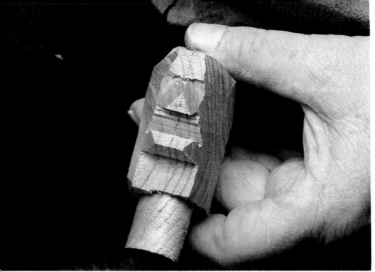

Move back to the nose and take it to this point.

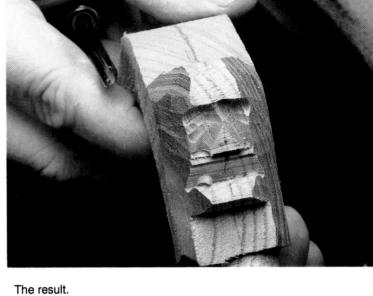

The result.

Come in from the outside with a gouge and open up the eye socket.

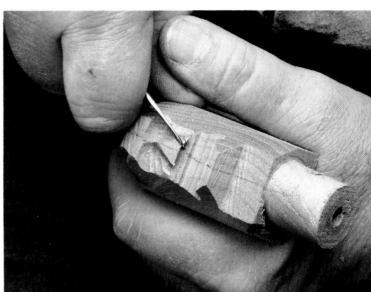

Cut in at the corner of the nose...

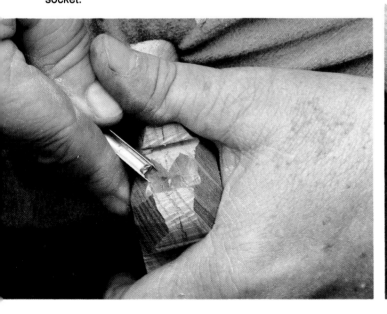

With the same gouge, come up beside the nose to the eye.

and back to it from the cheek for the nostril.

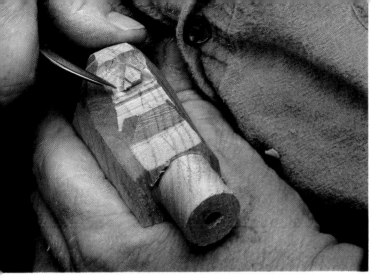

Do the same on the other side.

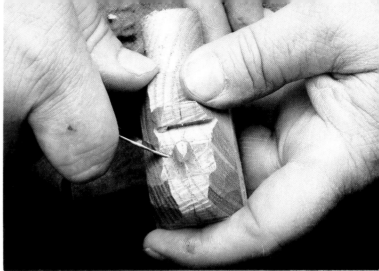

and down the cheek line. This is a double forty-five degree angle, 45 degrees down the face and 45 degrees in.

The result.

Cut back from the lip at a 45 degree angle to complete the triangle. The nitch should fall out.

To define the cheek cut in beside the nose...

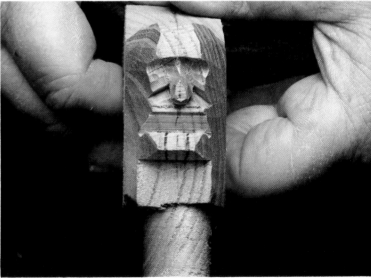

The result. I've drawn the line for the width of the pipe below the nose at the chin.

Cut a stop in the line of the pipe...

Clean up the cuts with a knife.

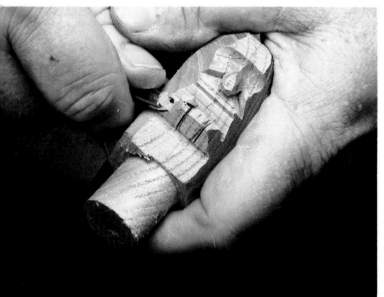

and come back to it with a gouge.

Draw in the pipe stem.

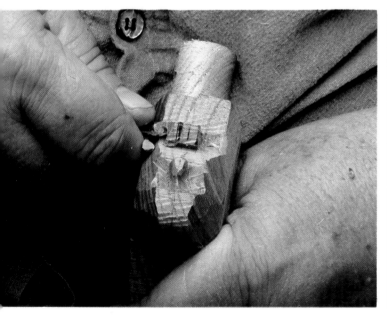

Repeat on the other side.

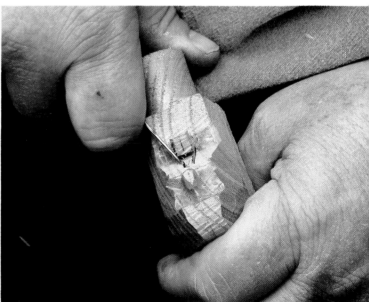

Cut a stop on each side...

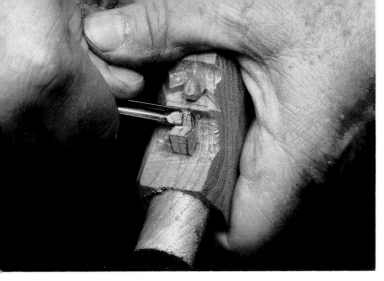

and come back to the stops with a gouge.

That brings the face to this point.

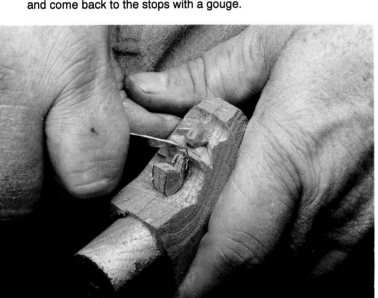

About now I need to decide what to do with the moustache. To begin with I will make two cuts at the bottom center of the moustache...

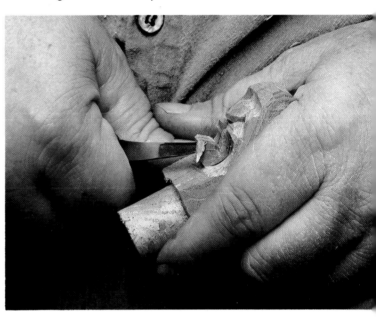

Knock the corners of the pipe bowl off to bring it to octagonal. I always go to an octagon shape before going to round because it helps keep things proportional.

and cut back to it from below, following the line of the pipe stem. This makes the stem look like it goes right into the mouth.

Shape the stem.

With the cup of the gouge against the face, come down over the cheek.

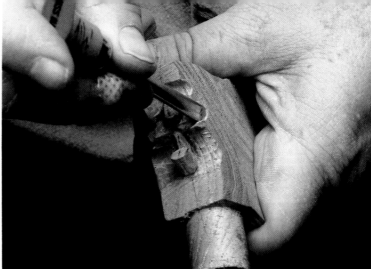

With the same gouge push in on the bottom line of the moustache. This should come around the side.

Now with the cup of the gouge facing out, come back to the cheek from the moustache.

This takes us to this point.

This gives it an exaggerated look to the cheeks that will be smoothed later.

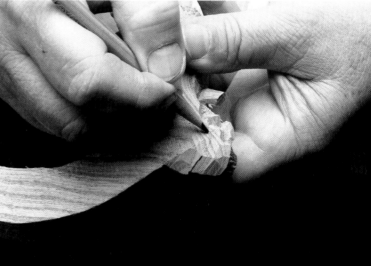

Draw the hairline, from the top of the bald head to the end of the sideburn.

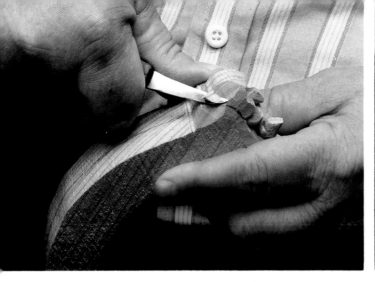

Cut from the line back toward the face.

With the same gouge come across the top of the eyebrows,

Round the forehead.

bringing them out.

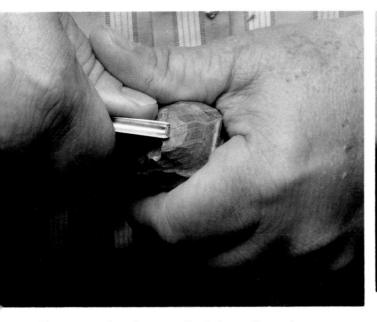

Use a gouge to get a separation between the eyebrows.

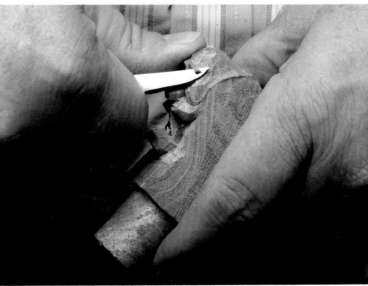

Narrow the temples at the corners of the eye. Simply start at the cheek and make a scooping cut up beside the eye.

A line from the eyebrow and the end of the nose will define the size and position of the ear. Draw the ear and the back of the side burn.

This creates the cup of the ear.

Cut a stop on the sideburn line...

Use a large veiner...

and come back to it with a gouge.

to trim around the ear.

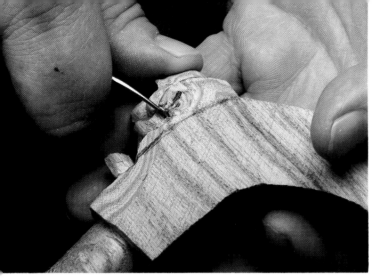

Cut down at the bottom of the sideburn...

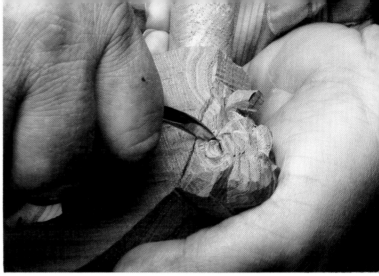

and here...

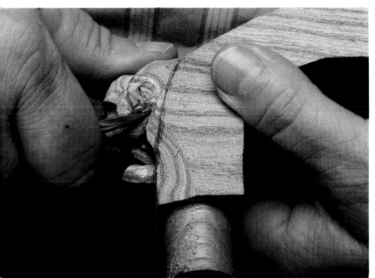

and back to it from the neck.

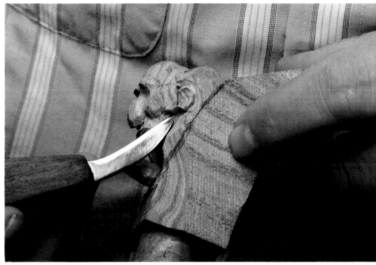

to remove a nitch that gives this result.

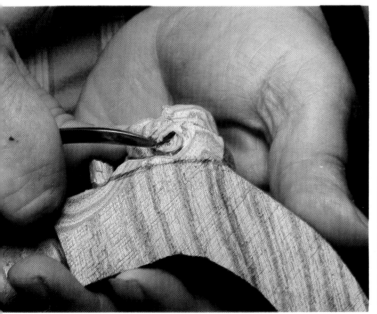

We need to separate the bottom of the ear from the end of the sideburn. Cut down here...

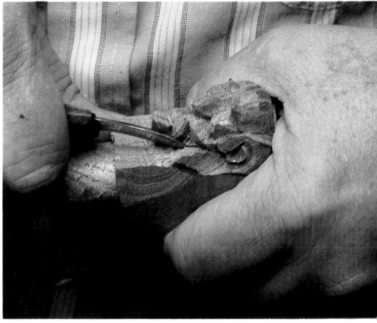

Cut a stop down the jaw line.

Cut back to it from the shoulder with a flatter gouge.

Continue the chin under the pipe by cutting along the chin line with the point of the knife...

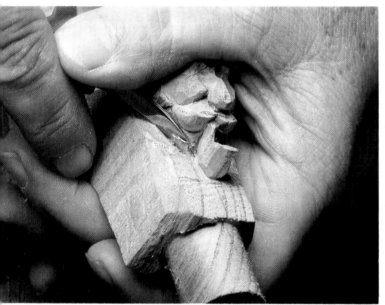

Create a chin by cutting down along the chin line

cutting along the line of the pipe...

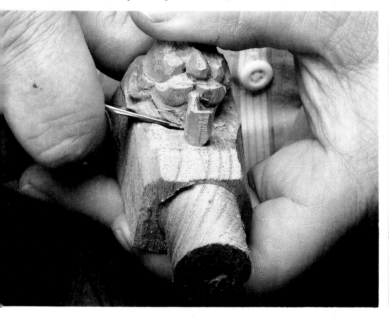

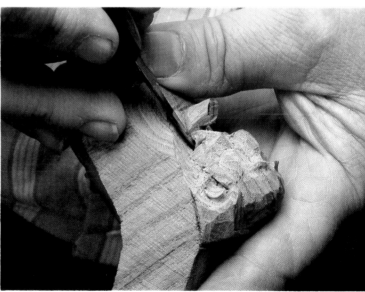

and back to it from the neck.

and cutting along the line of the chest.

This will pop out a triangular nitch. Repeat the process to deepen the cut and do the same thing on the other side until you work your way through.

Another view of progress.

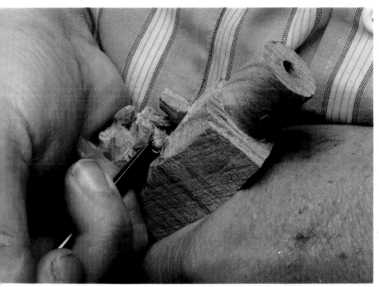

Come back and trim the side of the face to make it more realistic looking.

The handle needs thinning.

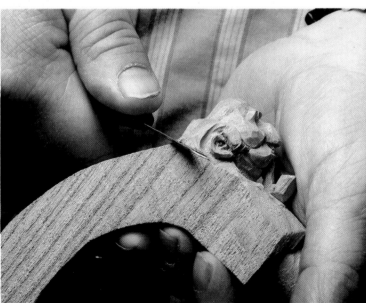

Progress.

At the back of the head cut a stop in the line of the cane...

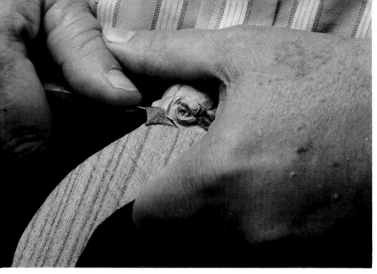

and down to it from the head.

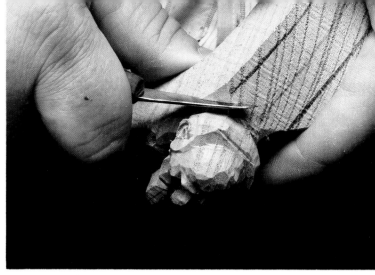

Begin to form a collar by cutting a stop...

Cut back along the stop and a nitch should pop out. Repeat this until the definition between the handle and the head is complete.

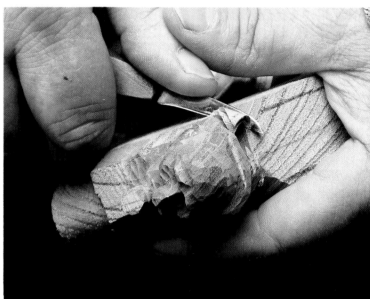

and trimming back to it from the handle.

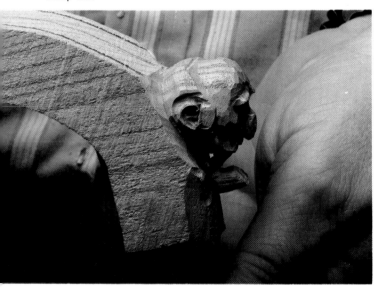

The result.

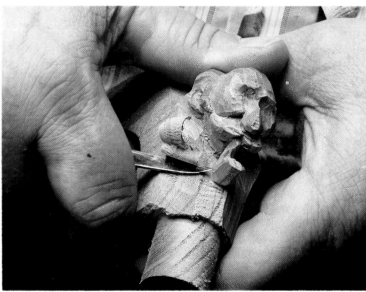

Knock the corners off the "chest" where it goes down to meet the cane.

Carry the line of the collar around to the front with a stop.

Trim back to it.

The collar is defined.

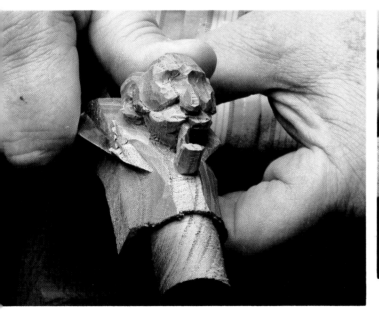

Repeat on the other side.

The detail of the ear is created with a small veiner, though a rotary tool would work well here. Simply make two holes, one at the top...

and one at the bottom.

The result.

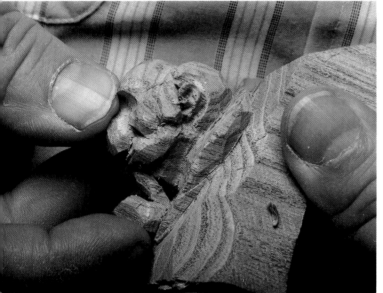

This takes you to this point.

The sleeve is a one-inch seamless brass tube cut with a tube cutter.

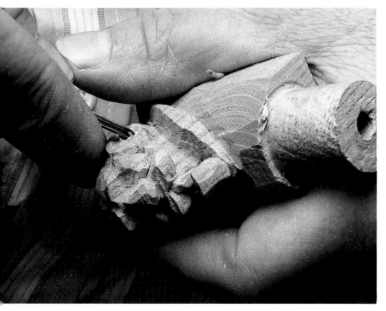

Then use the same tool to go around the rim of the ear.

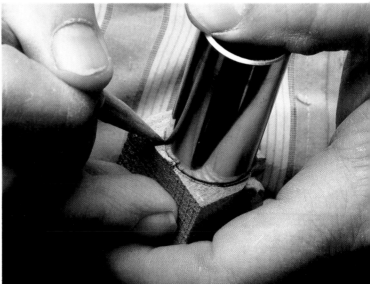

Mark the circumference on the handle.

Trim down to the circumference, beginning by knocking off the corners.

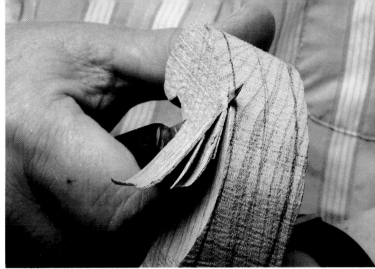

Narrow the handle. Take it to square first. Your goal is to get the handle as comfortable as possible.

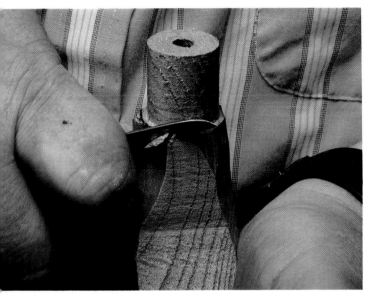

Then finish rounding it off.

Knock off the corners to take the handle to octagon.

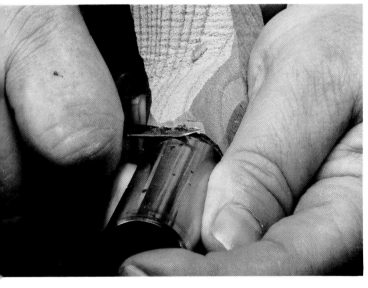

When it is roughly sized you can hold the brass in place to insure a flush cut. Be careful not to cut into the brass. It will dull your knife.

Everything in now octagonal.

I use a rotary tool with a small ball bit to make the hole for the pipe.

Add some lines to the moustache.

Add some hair lines to the sideburns. It is best to come from the back of the sideburn up to the face.

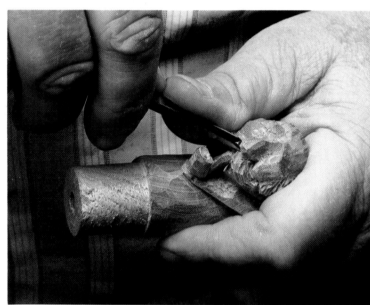

Come into the nostril with a small half-round gouge, with the cup side toward the lip.

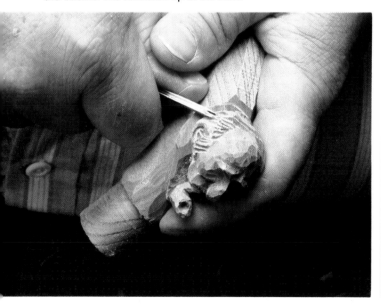

Continue over the top of the head.

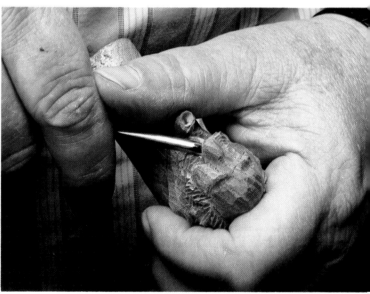

Do the same on the other side.

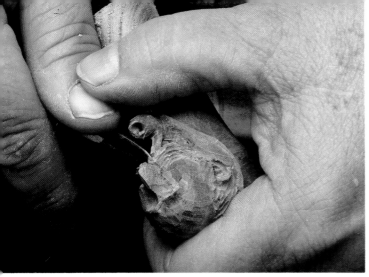

Clean the nostril out with a knife.

Pick an eyepunch that seems about the right side.

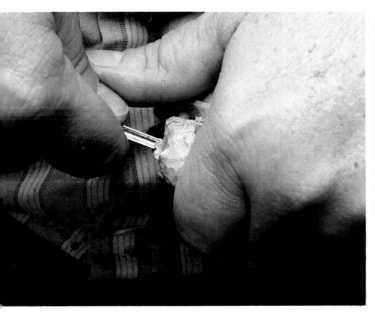

With the same half round, come over the top of the nostril on the outside to give it some flare.

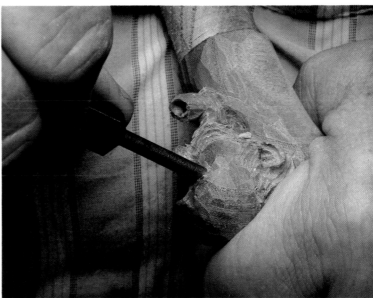

Starting with the left eye, push and turn the punch to create the eye.

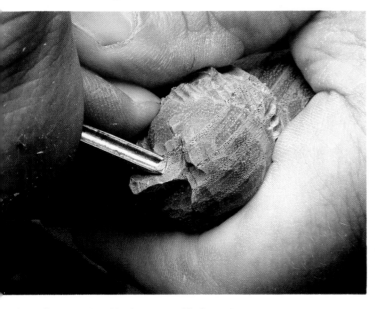

Come up beside the nose with the same gouge.

This rubber piece on the end makes the eyepunch a much more comfortable tool to use. You can get one at almost any hardware store.

Do the right eye to get to this point.

With a knife, cut along the top eyelid into the corner of the eye.

Do the same along the bottom eyelid.

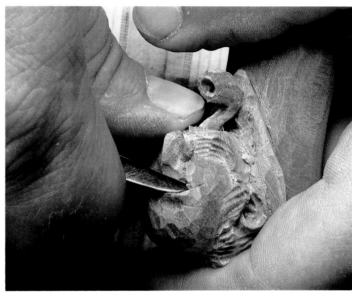

Now with your blade flat against the eyeball, push it into the corner. A triangular nitch should pop out.

Repeat on the other side.

22

Sand the handle. I use a bow sander.

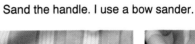

The finished face.

Take the octagonal handle to round.

The finished handle.

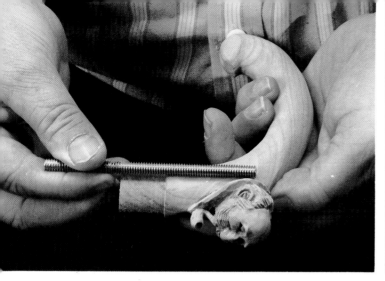

You want the threaded rod to go deeply into the cane so it picks up the strength of the grain. Go as far as you can without breaking through.

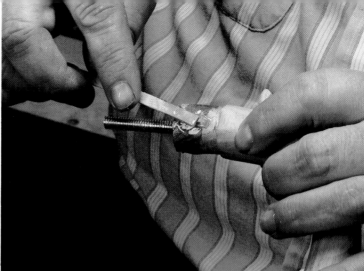

Put epoxy around the collar of the handle.

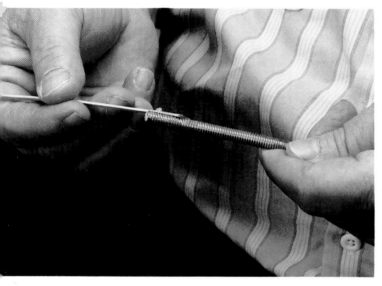

Work epoxy into the threads of the screw.

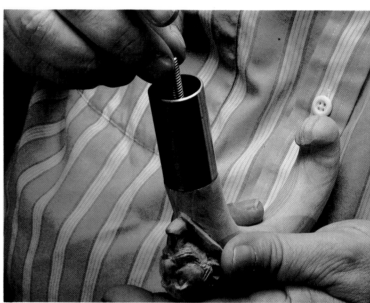

Put the brass cuff in place and let it set up.

Screw the rod into the place. The hole should be as big as the center of the rod, but not as big as the threads.

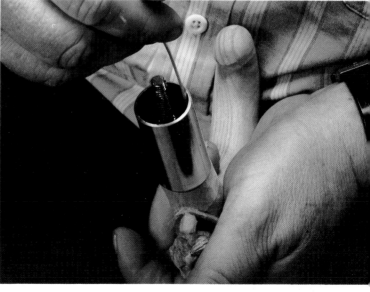

When it is set apply epoxy to the exposed portion of the threaded rod and to the inside of the brass cuff.

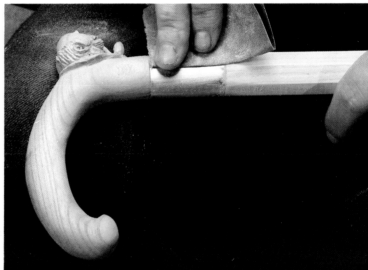

Sand around and over the cuff. The sanding gives the brass a nice antiqued look.

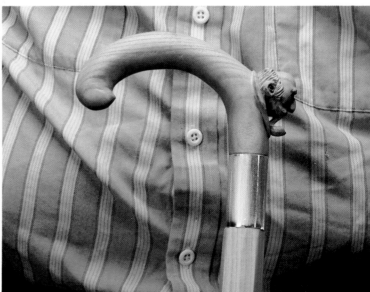

Connect the stick to the handle assembly and clamp it so it sets straight. A word about the stick. For years I could not find a source for cane sticks so I would make my own using a nice piece of wood and a drawknife or a lathe. I have recently found a commercial source, which is a cane company that manufactures stock canes for stock yards. The cane stick should be plenty long for comfort.

Go over it with a finer piece of sandpaper.

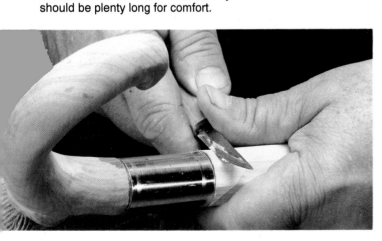

After the cane is set, round the top half inch or so of the stick to the cuff.

Ready for finishing.

If epoxy gets on the wood be sure to remove it or the stain won't penetrate.

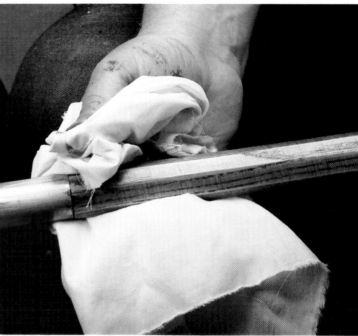

Polish it with a clean cloth.

The stain/finish I am using is Briwax™ which is a mixture of carnauba and bee's wax and stain. It is applied with steel wool. Rub it right into the wood. Other stains well also work, so use one you like.

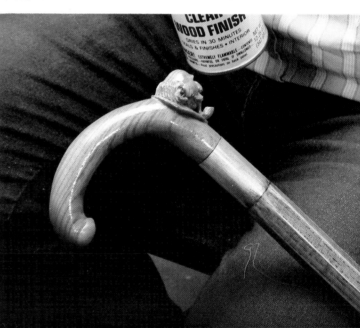

Apply spray to the handle. Let it dry and reapply. Continue the process until you are satisfied with the finish.

Rub in a second coat with a rag.

Carving the Antler Cane

The synthetic horn may carve with a knife, but for this project and I will use a rotary tool. Begin with a steel burr bit to round of the corners. I would use a rotary tool on real antler as well.

On the right is a cane from carved natural deer antler. In North Carolina and some other states it is illegal to sell animal parts, so antler is not available unless you are a hunter or know someone who will give it to you. The only alternative for cane making is to use a casted antler. An unfinished cast horn is at the left, and the center piece is cast and then finished with stain. This cast antler is actually easier to carve than bone, and just as durable. The stained casted antler is what we will use for this project.

Round all around the butt of the antler.

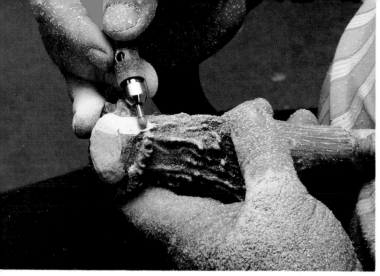

This area will become the face, so I want to knock a little bit off.

In drawing I want to take advantage of the ridge for the nose.

Progress.

Here you can see the center line, the brow, and the nose drawn.

With the same ball bit, carve out the eye socket.

Do the same on the other side of the nose.

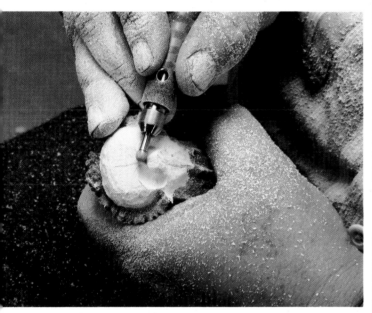

Come lightly across the bridge of the nose.

Progress.

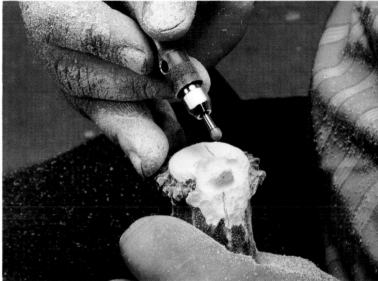

Come under the nose and round it off.

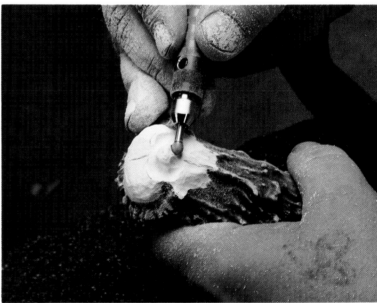

Push in to form a hint of the nostril.

Come down the side of the moustache. I'm going to tie it in with the ridge on the raw antler.

Carry the lines of the moustache into the antler. They will be the underside of the moustache.

Do the same on the other side, again taking advantage of any natural ridges.

Bring some whisker lines down from the mouth.

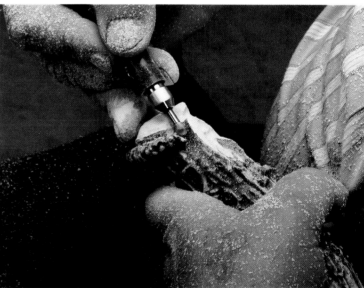

Start a mouth.

I need to widen the face, which I do by cutting a little more of the antler off at the cheek.

Do the same on the other side to keep balance.

Cut a groove over the eyebrow.

Carry the eye sockets around into the temple. This will bring out the cheek.

Blend the forehead into the groove.

Do the same on the other side.

Separate the eyebrows.

31

Progress.

and right, top...

Switch to a smaller steel burr and deepen the nostrils.

and bottom.

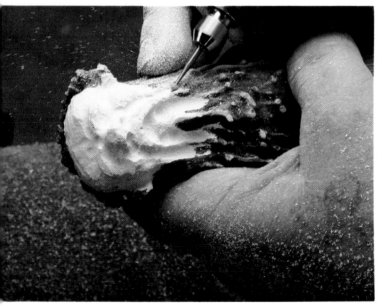

Deepen the lines of the moustache left...

Come under the bottom lip to bring out the mouth.

32

Come over the top of the nostril to create the flare.

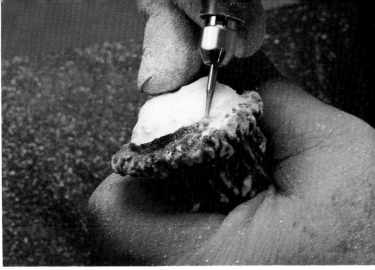

Go around the hairline, taking the stain off the smooth part, but leaving the ring of outcroppings intact.

The smaller bit basically takes the same lines and deepens and increase them, like here at the bridge of the nose.

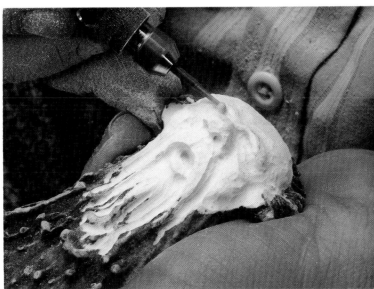

Go under the brow and create eyelids.

Separate between the sides of the moustache.

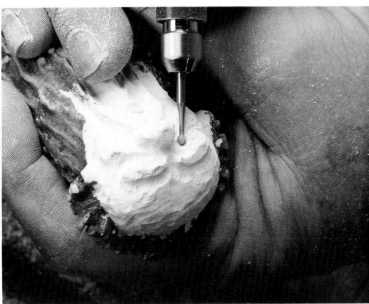

Go back under the lid and create the eye.

Close-up of the eyes and the mouth.

Shape the nose.

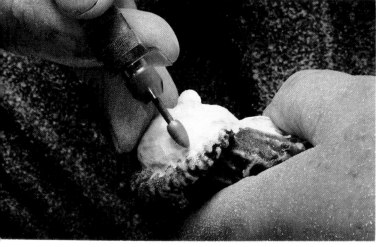

Switch to a ruby cone bit for smoothing.

Once you get your major lines it's just a matter of going back and refining them.

Progress.

Switch to a finer diamond bit. Add hairs to the eyebrows...

and the beard.

the moustache...

Some fine single strands of hair going into the antler add life to the character.

the "mane"...

For even finer work I use a bit with an edge that I can use for creating a very thin groove.

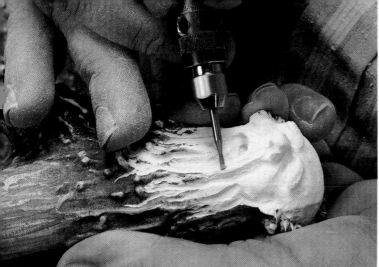

This will create even smaller, more detailed features.

Cut into the eye for the pupil.

A sharp, pointed bit...

Finished.

will help me bring out the eyes.

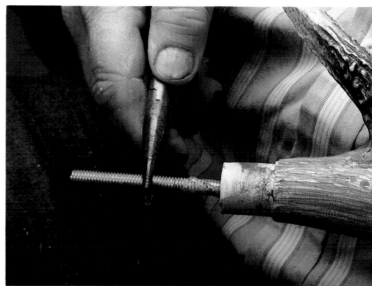

Mount the handle in the same way as the other cane. Apply epoxy to the threaded rod and screw it into place.

Apply glue to the collar of the handle

I will sand the aluminum cuff to give it the antiqued look.

Put the cuff on. For this cane it is a one inch anodized aluminum tube about two inches long. Let the glue set before applying the stick.

The Briwax works as an antiquing agent for the handle. Apply with a stiff bristled brush.

When the glue is set, put the handle on the stick. This is a found stick.

Wipe off immediately.

If it is too dark a little turpentine on the brush will clean it up
real good.

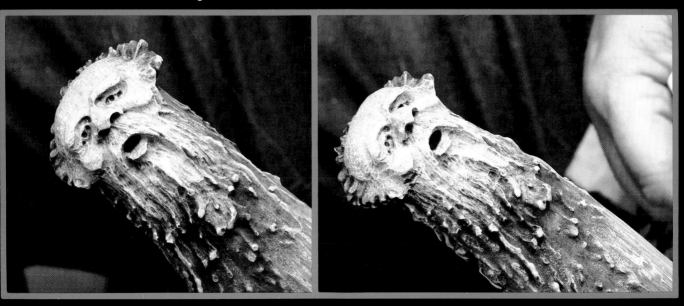

Buff it with a cloth to get this nice antiqued finish. Now we can
see all the detail of the carving. With the white casting
material it is hard to see without it, both with the eye and the

The Gallery

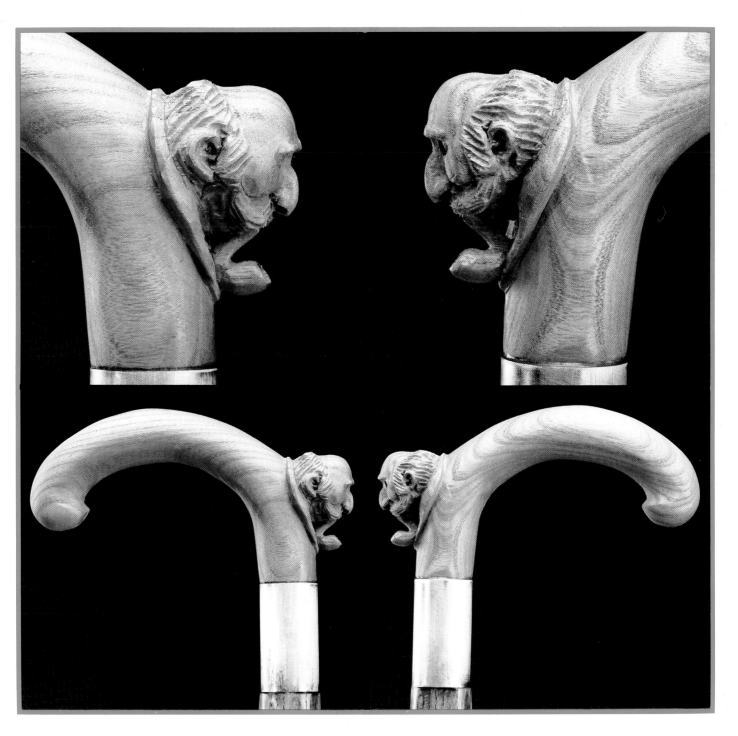

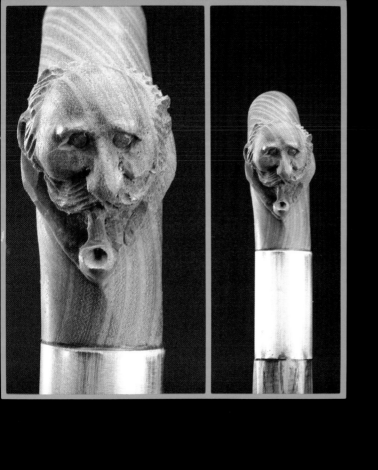

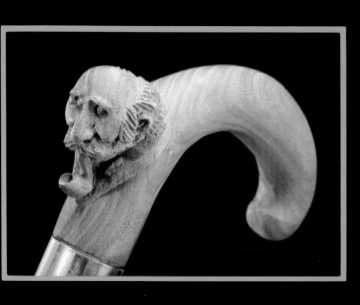

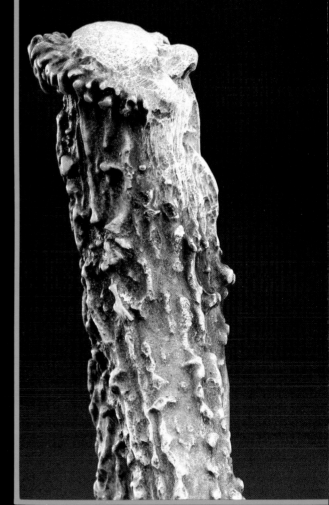

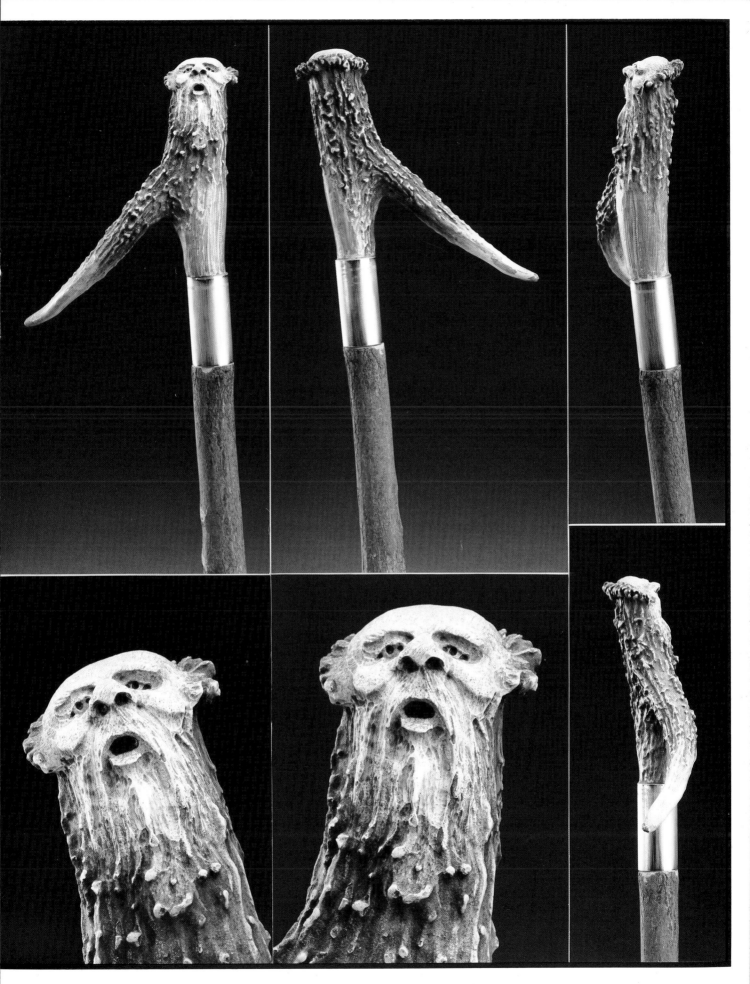

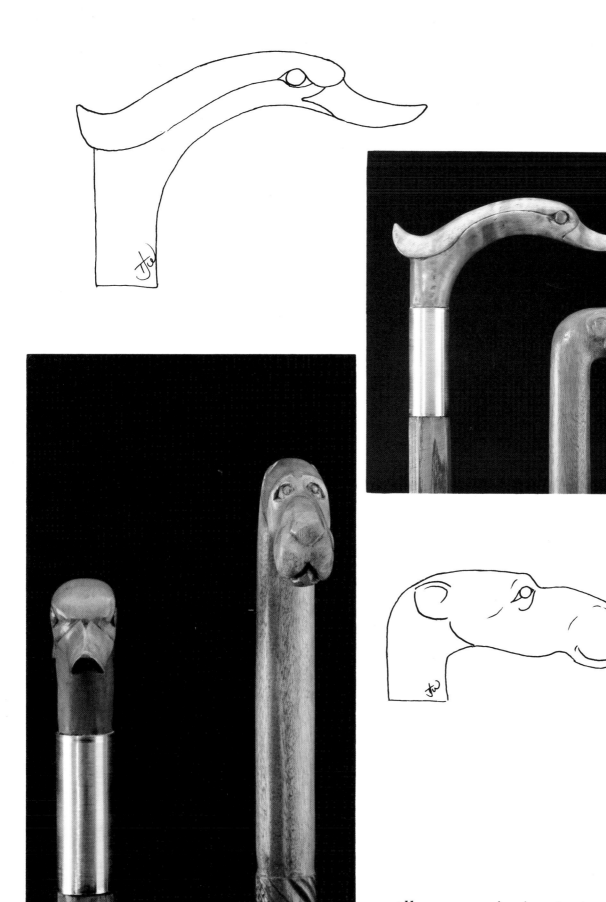

All patterns reduced to **65 %**.
Enlarge to **155%** for original size.

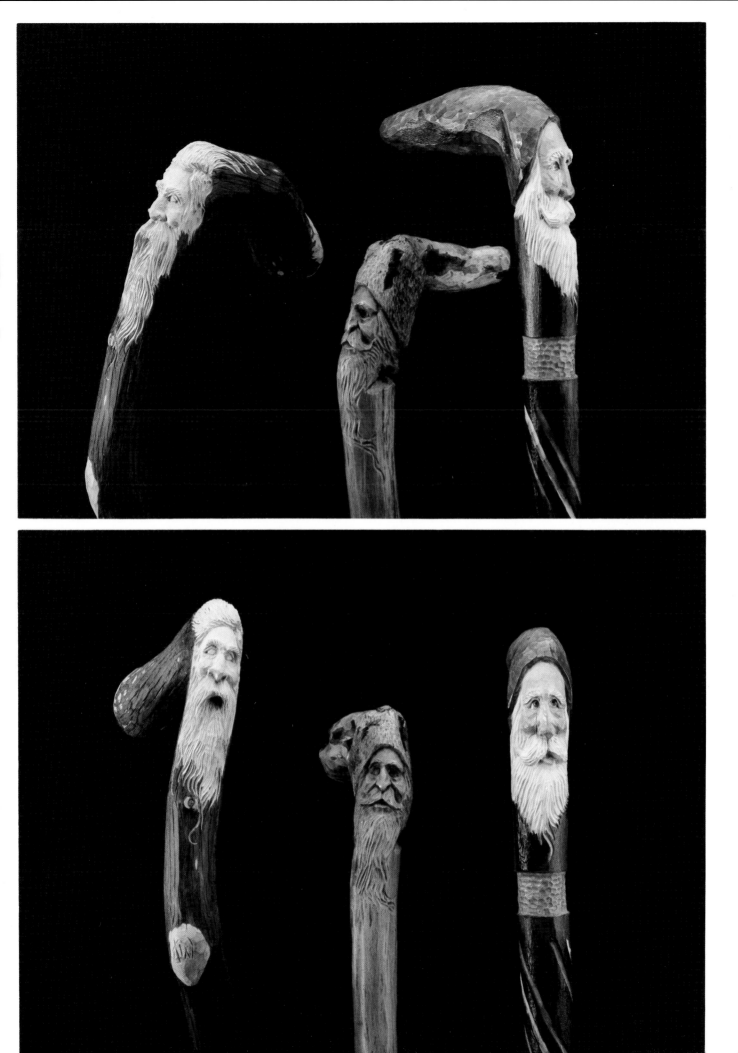

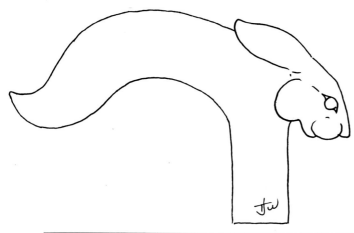

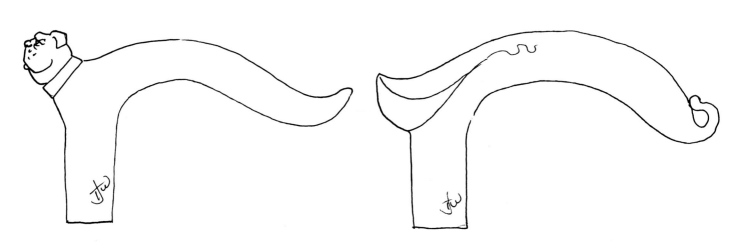

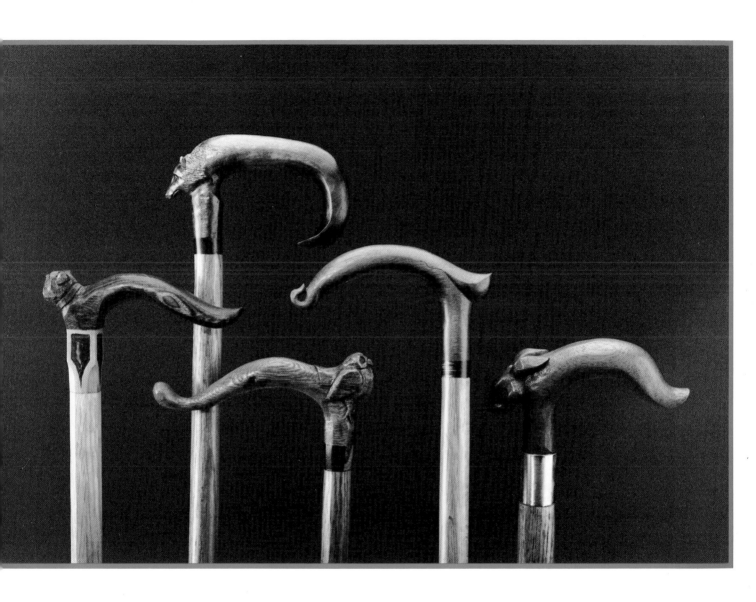

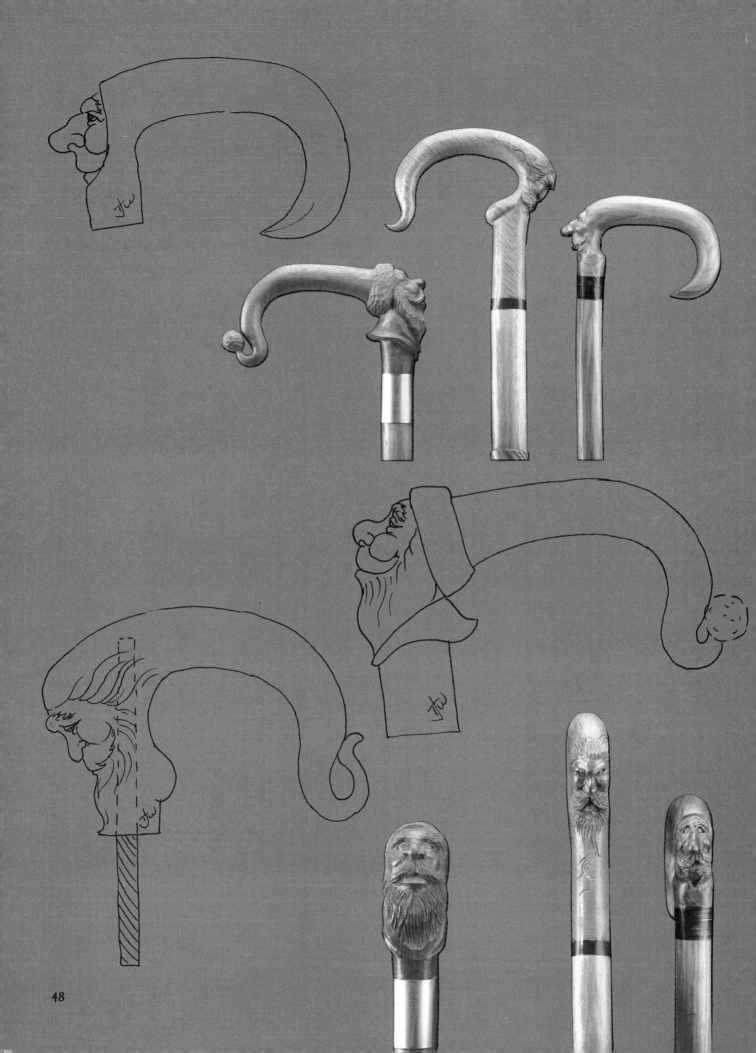